Life, Leadership & Success

Purposeful Life Lessons and Strategies for Managing Teams with Impact

CHARLIE NEWCOMB

Life, Leadership & Success:
Purposeful Life Lessons and Strategies for
Managing Teams with Impact

Paperback ISBN:979-8-89576-088-8
Hardback ISBN: 979-8-89576-089-5

Published by:

For Mom, always silently watching me grow and my biggest cheerleader!

Table of Contents

Introduction

"The past is for lessons, not for rehashing or reasons to go down again and defeat helplessly. The present is for debriefing what went on, what was learned, and what can be done differently in the future. What was learned and what can be done differently in the future."
—Unknown

I magine loving every single job you've ever had—sounds amazing, right? That's been my journey through four unique professional roles. Only a handful get to say they genuinely enjoy their work. Now, it's my turn to pay it forward and share the tools, skills, and knowledge that have fueled my passion. Ready to embark on your fulfilling career path? Let's make it happen together!

What some want, others want nothing to do with. What works for some doesn't work for others. Finding the right fit for your unique skills and interests is critical to personal and professional fulfillment. For me, performing a mundane job is something I never would succeed at. No two days have ever been the same in my line of work out of all the jobs I have experienced.

I greatly respect those who excel in routine, but it's not for me. As the year passes, I see too many assistant managers stocking pharmacy shelves or doing a complete stock reset at a sporting goods store.

However, I've realized my strengths and passions lie in work that brings something new and different daily. I learned at a young age that I belong in the service and sales industries and interact with people.

I thrive on variety and the excitement of tackling fresh challenges. I also need customer interaction, consistent personal and career growth, and dynamic environments.

After 33 years at McDonald's, I spent three years at A.J. Antunes. Next, I worked for six years at H+K International, which led me to where I am now: Manitowoc Ice. Pentair purchased Manitowoc Ice in July 2022, but I still work under the Manitowoc name.

In my third job since leaving McDonald's, the level and thoroughness of training I received there is second to none. I feel truly blessed to have found my way inside a company many perceive as a dead-end "McJob," a term that gained popularity in the early 2000s.

Dictionary.com defines "McJob as "an unstimulating, low-wage job with few benefits, especially in a service industry." My story will exemplify how the contrary became a reality for me.

The term "McJob" reminds me of a parent event at my daughter's elementary school. Several parents and I visited our kids' classrooms to discuss our careers. It was a wonderful chance to share our stories and experiences and give the students insight into various careers. I was excited to tell them about my work history and how I got to where I am today.

The talk went well, and the kids seemed genuinely engaged and interested. The students asked thoughtful questions, and right in front of my eyes, I could happily see a few of them considering a path they hadn't before. Thinking my story might inspire them to explore new possibilities was rewarding.

Unfortunately, things took a disappointing turn after we left. I later learned from my daughter that the teacher had negative words to say about my career. He told the kids my work was unreliable and said it was not as respectable as more traditional professions. Of course, there were some inaccurate statements about the industry, painting it negatively, like the phrase "McJob" and that all we do is flip burgers. I have learned to avoid negative people as they either have a problem or look negatively at other areas in life.

Hearing this was disheartening. While everyone is entitled to their opinion, sharing misinformation and undermining someone else's experiences is unacceptable. To dismiss our careers was not disrespectful to us and misleading to the kids.

I was disturbed by the teachers' mockery of the fast food industry, suggesting, "You'll spend the rest of your life flipping burgers."

Feeling mixed emotions and ultimately bothered by the situation, I took action to help change an incorrect narrative. I didn't tell my daughter then, but I wrote a letter to her teacher the next day to share my perspective.

A position at McDonald's can provide an array of solutions:

- An entry-level position for a student.

- An excellent part-time job for a parent while their child is at school.
- A part-time hustle in your retirement years to help occupy your time.
- A second job to help pay for a dream vacation.
- For me, it is a rewarding career that I will forever cherish.

As a result, the teacher stopped referring to McDonald's jobs as just people who are "flipping burgers."

McDonald's started as a job while I was in college, and it unexpectedly started turning into a career slowly but surely. Not only did I receive excellent training, but it also taught me many life lessons that I will discuss in this book. If you have met me in the last 25 years, this may sound odd, but I was an introvert when I started at McDonald's.

Everything started to change when McDonald's recognized my potential. I began coming out of my shell, which eventually led to my being promoted to Assistant Manager. They even paid my enrollment fee to attend a Dale Carnegie course—talk about an employer going all-in on your development. I still remember the first-class lesson from this workshop.

The opening lesson focused on individual names, explicitly learning, remembering, and using people's names when speaking. I continue to apply this principle today, ensuring everyone is familiar with one another. I train everyone to achieve this and stress its importance.

I was recently at a meeting in Boston with a couple of former colleagues at H+K. At some point, I came across a fellow competitor and supplier vendor from my time with McDonald's.

I said to this gentleman, "Does everybody know Andrew and Thomas? Have you guys met each other?" Far too often, if you're ever conversing with three or four people, all parties aren't yet acquainted.

The person who doesn't know the others always feels awkward and uneasy. Think about how it makes you feel when someone remembers your name and speaks to you using your name. The little things go a long way -using names, looking people in the eyes, and not making people feel like a third wheel. Take an interest in them with simple questions; an easy place to start is asking about their job.

Doing all those things is valuable, but there is always room for improvement. Engaging in a conversation that includes all parties can relate to quickly drops communication barriers. I wish all company training would involve acknowledging and remembering names.

When you meet a new colleague or manager from another company, do not assume they will remember your name the next time you meet, whether in a week, month, or year, as it could make for an uncomfortable situation. Simply reintroduce yourself again: "Hi, my name is Charlie, in case you forgot. We met last year." Have you ever walked away from somebody, turned to a co-worker, and said, "I wish I remembered his name?"

Throughout the years, I've learned numerous lessons, some more challenging to grasp than others; in November 2001, McDonald's Corporation downsized for the first time. This change removed many hardworking people from their positions, forever changing corporate life, in my opinion.

McDonald's Corporation wanted to eliminate the bottom 20% of performers. For years after this, until I left, I constantly looked over my shoulder, awaiting somebody to come along and tell me I was out of a job. If you are or were working in the McDonald's world, you may be able to relate to this thought: there is or was nowhere to go after McDonald's. I am here to tell you there is.

I'll share how I navigated that experience to assist others facing similar challenges. Additionally, I'll explore my story, experiences, and the lessons I've learned over 30+ years as a leader in a management role. If you are a manager at any level or aspire to lead and make a difference in your workplace, this book is for you. This book distinguishes itself from other leadership and training guides by blending professionalism with humor and a soothing tone.

In my opinion, corporate training has become very weak in the past ten years. This book will help you combat that problem, providing powerful real-life experiences that can help you become a better boss and a more robust manager.

Have you ever traveled down a path you thought was yours but made a U-turn? You're not alone; we often don't know until we try.

CHAPTER 1

The Beginning

"Progress, far from consisting in change, depends on retentiveness. When change is absolute, there remains no being to improve, and no direction is set for possible improvement, and when experience is not retained, as among savages, infancy is perpetual. Those who cannot remember the past are condemned to repeat it.

In the first stage of life, the mind is frivolous and easily distracted; it misses progress by failing in consecutiveness and persistence. This is the condition of children and barbarians, in whom instinct has learned nothing from experience."
— *George Santayana.*

As my senior year of high school neared its end in the spring of 1979, I felt excited and uncertain about my future. Graduation was a chance for new beginnings, but saying goodbye to the life I had known, friends, and familiar places was hard. Like some of you reading on, I had stronger family relationships than others, with mom being the most brutal goodbye after graduation.

Walking across the commencement stage felt like stepping into an unknown world where my reality and dreams would soon meet. The world seemed full of possibilities, and I was ready to start the next chapter. The question was, what would this next chapter hold? I was a typical 18-year-old overwhelmed by transitioning from a structured high school schedule to figuring it out independently.

In September 1979, I packed my bags and traveled to the University of Maine, Orono, to major in Computer science. I had never been in love with this subject, but it seemed more interesting than the others. I expected to attend college, so I chose this major because it was the best option.

As eager as I was to move away from home to attend college and start post-high school life, I quickly and often questioned whether it was the right decision and wasn't sold that it was my endgame. After my first semester, I decided to make it my last because I didn't know what I truly wanted my next step to be. I couldn't warrant spending money on an uncertain future, so I ultimately decided to follow a different path because something didn't feel right. Whether it was:

- The struggle with the new independence and the intensive demands of balancing academics and personal life
- Questioning if this decision aligned with my career goals
- Homesickness, or
- The pressure to succeed.

It is interesting how much can change in a few short months. My dorm room, which once felt like an exciting, brand-new start, became a chapter I was eager to close. I was leaving behind the familiar routine of classes and campus life to explore a way of life that lined up with what was best for me. It was a bold move, driven by the hope that something better awaited me beyond those college walls. Even though it was a scary decision, I was comfortable with it.

I rode my bike to McDonald's in Westbrook, Maine, shortly after returning from my lone college semester to apply for a job. Even though I applied, I felt my main focus and calling was enlisting in the military.

With my full-time academic route on hold, my next step seemed clear in February 1980: joining the United States Air Force. I wanted to enlist in this military branch because of its highly sought-after MP, or Military Police, Program. While this seemed like an excellent decision for my life, I received a phone call that changed everything shortly before I committed. I mean, it changed everything. I received a phone call from McDonald's about the job application I had submitted two weeks prior.

I ended the conversation initially because I was determined to enlist in the military. As I had time to reflect, my plans shifted because I still felt uncertain about my future. Here I was, beating myself up about the enormous pressure of "what I would do with my future." Sure enough, I picked up the phone, called McDonald's back, and accepted the interview. It wasn't the path I had imagined, but it was a HUGE step forward and an opportunity to figure out my next move.

When I walked into the interview, I felt a mix of determination and nerves. I felt more confident than ever because I had a smoking ace - I was lucky enough to get interviewed by a classmate and friend in my graduating class. Although it felt much longer, just a few days later, I received a call with the incredible news that they had offered me a position. From here, it was off to the races! I carried the momentum of this victory into holding myself accountable to continue pursuing my education simultaneously.

After accepting this offer, my plans of entering the Air Force were dead. I was ecstatic to learn that I could earn police training while going to school and working at McDonald's. Although it wasn't military training, it perfectly fit my situation. I was also relieved I didn't need to enlist in the military to study police training.

In what turned out to be an eventful month, I elected to study Criminal Justice at Southern Maine Vocational Technical Institute at the end of February. After finishing my morning classes, I typically spent my days working from 12 PM to 7 PM. I could work 25-30 hours per week while tending to my studies.

Was my future slightly delayed compared to the rest of my graduate class? Sure, by roughly a year and a half. It's a good thing that it's not about where you start or how long it takes you to figure it out but where you finish.

I started working at McDonald's on March 10, 1980, and evolved within the company culture more than I could have imagined. From my very first day, I LOVED working for this company. It allowed me to enter the real world and pay the bills. The 4-mile bike ride to work at 5 AM prepared me to be my best mentally each day. I rode my bike to work daily as a crew member from the day they hired me through June.

I loved it even when I started at the bottom—learning the ins and outs of the company—and was eager to prove myself as a crew member. Writing this book brings me joy, including how I evolved from a $3.10 hourly employee to helping lead the company in impactful and meaningful ways.

I kid you not; on my first day, I accidentally burned three fingers while using the grill for the first time! Despite a more challenging start than anticipated, I was determined not to give up.

As a low-shift runner, I first met Steve Walach, a new supervisor for my store's area. Steve became a very influential mentor and friend in my life. We are still friendly today, and he is still with the company in a different capacity as a Franchisee. You will soon learn how large a role he played in my life.

> *"Stay close to people who inspire you to be better,*
> *hold you accountable, believe in your dream,*
> *and lift you up.*
> *— @riseinspiredwoman*

In just a few short months, in June 1980, through hard work and accountability, I was soon offered a promotion to Shift Manager. This position is also known as a lower-level manager or swing manager, and I began this role at the same store where I started. With this promotion, I was able to buy my first car. I loved my Ford Granada for $4,200.

With my promotion to shift manager, I would now lead anywhere from 10 to 15 employees on each shift as the on-duty manager. When you are promoted to Assistant Manager, you'll receive the exclusive McOpCo designation, indicating your affiliation with the corporate team. To clarify, McOpCo stands for McDonald's Operating Company. As a shift manager, you manage only in the store where you received training.

In September 1980, I began studying Criminal Justice part-time at SMVTI, marking the unexpected beginning of this company. After grinding for four months, I earned the chance to take on more responsibility. Looking back, I fell into this job, and this promotion was the beginning of something incredible because it was perfect alignment:

- I love working for people with a vision.
- I love working with people and the teamwork element.
- I loved the fun atmosphere.
- I loved that each day was different; it never became mundane.

As I learned more about the company and business, I began to love all the other areas even more:

- I learned to love large amounts of responsibility and leading by example
- The sense of teamwork
- How profitability affects a business
- The little things I could do to improve the customer experience
- How decisions made affect the entire company

McDonald's has been very gracious to me since my first day. This promotion helped me improve in a critical area - my confidence. Admittedly, I was nervous in my initial interactions with customers, but being promoted helped improve my confidence in ways I never thought possible.

Have you ever been at a drive-thru and had an employee ask you to park outside because your food wasn't ready yet? Until recently, a third window in the line wasn't an option. When I first started working there, this was my worst-case scenario. I dreaded having to have this awkward conversation with customers. However, with longer shifts and more of them over time, I enjoyed talking and interacting with customers more and more. As a byproduct, my confidence and leadership abilities improved.

I began to ponder, did I have more than a job, but a long-term career opportunity right before me? Upon this realization, I had a great career opportunity I never took for granted. This opportunity also helped mend a problematic relationship with my father; some of you reading about it may relate to having a supporting father but disagree on the direction of your life.

He loved that I was going to the service, but he was distraught when I decided against enlisting to work part-time. Soon enough, his mind was changed when he found out I was working at McDonald's. He began raving about my decision once I grew into a management position at a Fortune 500 company. He understood the stock market very well and loved McDonald's as a company. I am proud to have learned that approximately only 40 companies are still on the Fortune 500 stock market from when they launched their IPO in the mid-1960s.

Around the world, McDonald's stores are run either by those who pay license fees to become franchisees or by corporate McDonald's, which owns roughly 6% of the national stores. If you walk into your local McDonald's, you cannot differentiate between a company-owned or franchise-owned store.

There is much more growth working for corporate McDonald's. Think of the Corporate McDonald's locations as the company's "farm team," similar to those in professional sports. They coach and train employees to help the company succeed at the next level and in the location where the employee can add the most value.

Trying too hard to impress Steve Walach, I received a failing grade on an evaluation. During a corporate three-day store assessment, also called a "Full Field Assessment," I failed the dinner shift evaluation on a Thursday night in November 1980. I was so nervous that I created a lot of chaos for the entire store. This was disheartening, and I felt like I let everybody in the store down.

After I stopped feeling sorry for myself, I decided to do everything within my power to be better at my job. I took on a new challenge to improve my shift running skills. One day, it just clicked. Suddenly, I was as confident as ever in my shift running skills.

Unannounced visits from Steve Walach went better, and he was starting to notice. With each small "win" like this, I became increasingly excited about my potential growth at McD's. It was time to show initiative and express my desire for a promotion to the next manager level. I knew I had to be proactive and clear my ambitions to the area supervisor.

In the spring of 1981, I had the opportunity to transfer to the South Portland Waterman Drive store. It was a move that would enhance my skills, and it was also easier to get to work from school. Another leading supporter in my life became this store's manager, Lisa. We immediately had a strong connection, which immensely helped me on my journey. Plus, she helped me by always putting in a good word for Steve Walach.

Lisa helped me with my issue of being too close to others, personally and professionally. I have always feared getting close to people, especially in my corporate life. As a supervisor, I couldn't get close to my managers because I was their boss.

That carried over into my life, and to this day, I'm still hesitant about making friends in the workplace and outside of work. I often see people today in the McDonald's world who are close to some of their managers, yet they're their bosses and hang out together outside of work. I've never been one to do that. I always felt a sense of a boss-subordinate relationship.

It was hard for me to take that leap of faith.

It's a matter of taking a chance and opening up to develop a level of trust, and admittedly, I neglected these opportunities over the years. With Lisa, I could recognize it and work towards making changes.

You give trust when meeting someone, but they can destroy it in a heartbeat, making it hard to rebuild. When you trust somebody without any doubts, and later, they go behind your back or break that trust, it casts doubt. These actions also lead to indecisions in other areas of life, making it difficult to regain confidence.

Whether you act deceitfully or take credit for the work you did, you can cause irreparable damage. Trust involves mutual respect, so treat others how you want to be treated.

Here is an example from my life: I met with the leadership team at work to try and change a process and brought in two of the group's leaders to help support me. They did the opposite and were argumentative, leading to a four-on-one conversation. I had to make an uncomfortable phone call the following day to ask why he had done the opposite and wasted our time, our most valuable asset. In this situation, a conflict occurred, and it was tough to regain the trust with the leadership team.

What is the difference between a high-trust and low-trust organization?

In high-trust environments, employees feel they can accomplish more with less. They feel empowered to act freely and to take risks. Let's dive deeper into work environments.

I found an interesting statistic from a study revealed in *Harvard Business Review*. Employees who work at high-trust companies report:

- 13% fewer sick days
- 29% more satisfaction in their lives
- 40% less burnout
- 50% higher productivity
- 74% less stress
- 76% more engagement, and
- 106% more energy at work than those working for low-trust companies

In environments where trust is low, the opposite effect emerges. Team members become bogged down by inter-office politics, leading to slower and less effective decision-making. Employees tend to withhold information and feel insecure about sharing it.

How do you change a low-trust environment to one of high caliber? You guessed it: effective leadership! That's where Lisa came in.

> *"Leadership is all about people. It is not about organizations, plans, or strategies. It is all about motivating people to get the job done. You have to be people-centered."*
> — *Colin Powell*

A work-related situation can become problematic if a relationship becomes overly friendly. The whole dynamic can shift, and not in a positive way.

After graduating from SMVTI in May 1982, I continued in the role for several months as I searched for opportunities in law enforcement.

I have always believed that everything happens for a reason. Soon enough, it all came together. After two failed interviews in the towns of Yarmouth, ME, and Falmouth, ME, I had an interview with the city of South Portland, ME. One of the captains interviewed me for my first interview, and I left feeling confident about how it went. Shortly after the interview, I got a letter requesting a second interview.

I vividly remember receiving the letter in the mail asking me to come back. Excited about earning another meeting and juggling school and part-time work, I made an error that changed the course of my life. I missed this job interview because I thought the letter said Thursday, but it was on Tuesday. There I was, classified as a "no show." When I realized my mistake, I felt upset and worried. However, I truly believe everything happens for a reason.

This was God's way of telling me to stay put. It became increasingly clear how much I loved working at McDonald's, and it may be the right place for me. The opportunity to grow was evident, so I thought it may be time to seize it.

Sometimes, life guides us to where we need to be, even if it doesn't initially seem that way. I also knew I could make more money working at McDonald's with a more robust career path, an overwhelming sign I couldn't ignore, so I continued working hard to become a Second Assistant.

> *"It's not WHERE you work,*
> *but WHO you work with that makes a job worth*
> *going to every day."*
> *— Anonymous*

I continued to hustle and help those around me succeed in earning my next promotion to Second Assistant at the St. John Street location. With this promotion, I moved to the St. John St. location in Portland, Maine, where Area Supervisor Steve Walach continued to notice my work. I was eager to learn; like Steve, he saw my potential. I focused on attention to detail, day-to-day operations, and providing next-level customer service. I never cared how many hours I worked and was committed to growth with the company.

As a Second Assistant Manager, you receive training in your current store and are expected to achieve significant growth. You then transfer to a different store location to advance to a

First Assistant. I started as a Second Assistant in March 1983 and was promoted to First Assistant in October 1985. Becoming a first assistant involved countless lessons learned and impactful moments, such as preparing for my Review Board.

To move up in the company, you must go to a Review Board with several supervisors to discuss your accomplishments. Operations Manager Charlie Strong had announced a State of Maine Challenge. You had to be the first store in Maine to achieve sales of 50% drive-thru for two consecutive months. Once the drive-thru concept began gaining momentum, even the best stores earned around 40%. Fast-forward 30 years, and some are up to nearly 80% in drive-thru traffic.

I remember Charlie talking about it all in a foreshadowing manner: the drive-thru will one day change the fast-food industry. He was sure right about that, among many other areas. The first drive-thru McDonald's opened in 1972 but wasn't widely known or used as often as today. The idea of a drive-thru was beginning to evolve.

He offered an incentive- dinner with the management team of the first store in the state that achieved drive-thru sales of 50% for two consecutive months. I took this as help and motivation to become a first assistant.

At Board Reviews, interviewees need to discuss many things, including:

- What are your action plans going forward?
- What did you do well?
- How did you do it?
- Which areas did you perform poorly in?

I needed to clarify to the board that I aspired to grow beyond a first assistant role and become a store manager. I succeeded in doing so, and I want to extend special thanks to the supervisors on the board who listened to my story and supported my growth within the company.

During the Board of Review, I confidently presented my case. I highlighted the skills I had developed, the challenges I had overcome, and how I improved our team's performance. I also shared my vision for the future and how I could contribute even more in a higher role. I was ecstatic to announce that the Portland, Maine, store achieved two consecutive months of 50% Drive-thru time. We celebrated with a well-earned dinner with Mr. Strong and the rest of the management team.

When a company promotes someone to First Assistant Manager, it usually sends them to a different store from their training location. From there, the growth plan consists of a store manager, area supervisor, field consultant, training consultant, and others in the corporate world. Once you become store manager, you become the point of contact for the Area Supervisor.

My most recent promotion transferred me to the South Portland, Maine, restaurant as a first assistant. Steve saw how much work and passion I poured into the job. My new manager was Arden Davis, but he was soon transferred to the store in Falmouth, Maine, so it was during this time that Steve took a chance on me. In May 1986, he promoted me to the restaurant manager position at the Gorham Road McDonald's in South Portland. I was focused on making the most of this opportunity to springboard my future.

Pictured here is Steve Walach. I give him all the credit helping me groom my career in the McDonald's system. He will always be one of the key people behind my success.

Pictured above is the Walach family after receiving the prestigious "Ronald Award," given annually to one operator for outstanding performance. Pictured left to right is his son Chris, wife Lynne, Steve, and his son Brian. I have known Lynne and the boys since their birth.

CHAPTER 2

My First Store

"There are three constants in life... change, choice, and principles."
—Stephen Covey

May 1986 started my next chapter, where each routine action now had a greater purpose and a clearer vision for the future. With these new responsibilities came a big decision for me that was not easy: moving for the job. Yet again, Steve took a chance on me, entrusting me to run a multi-million-dollar restaurant.

On my first day as a new store manager, I felt a mixture of anticipation, excitement, and nervousness. My stride felt more confident, and my posture a bit taller as I took in the new reality of my role.

My dedication to the company, willingness to learn and be coachable, and hard work separated me from my peers. At just 25 years old, I earned this promotion to restaurant manager. It was uncommon for someone to only be in the First Assistant role for six months in 1986.

To be chosen, even while splitting responsibilities with another first assistant and over another high-performing one in the area, humbled me, and I was honored. Winning the National Science Fair was a unique achievement; I am still proud. Let's dive deeper.

Traditionally, managers send employees to different stores upon receiving this promotion. A newly promoted employee takes over when a manager moves on from their location. I was fortunate enough to continue building relationships with the same team.

Two other first assistants had already put in three years of service. One of the assistants, Harold, was upset he didn't get the promotion because he was in my store. I had to recognize his disappointment and give him time to work through it. Early jealousy eventually disappeared, and we had a great working relationship. Over time, we developed an excellent working relationship, and he became a fantastic assistant manager. This experience taught me valuable lessons in conflict resolution, as some others also initially struggled to see me as the leader. I had to earn respect at each step of the way.

With this promotion, animosity was also built with other co-workers. At the same time, I was expected to take charge, delegate, and improve operations immediately. The existing staff views the individual as an authoritative figure in their leadership role and immediately gains their respect. Once you wear the manager hat, all eyes are on you, and you are putting your foot down about any changes coming forward.

As a new boss, it's crucial to acknowledge your challenges and the discomfort people may feel around you. Ideally, no team members would leave, but your responsibility is to build a team that believes in you. Those who don't align with your vision and the company culture may not be the best fit for your store.

Staffing is traditionally difficult to maintain in quick-service environments. Chances are, you are already short-staffed, so it is vital to retain as many employees as possible for as long as possible. I worked hard each day to earn the respect of my staff while being short-staffed. As you build trust with your team and care for them as people, a goal of mine was to improve staffing turnover.

A few techniques have helped me lead in this area throughout my career. I had to think quickly as I was no longer the Assistant Manager who would seek answers from the restaurant manager. I was the manager, and my co-workers expected me to provide all the answers.

As I led my teams, it was important to identify the root causes of the restaurant's opportunities and problems. Some employees are unhappy about personal issues, while others may be upset with the workload or environment. Once you can address the problems, you can work together to find an effective solution.

After determining the cause, regular check-ins are vital to maintaining their happiness and growth. Provide constructive feedback and encourage honest feedback in return.

With this mutual feedback, the two of you can work on improving their growth trajectory with the company. With additional training, you can offer opportunities for skill development and career advancement. Ideally, a mentor/mentee relationship is formed like the one Steve and I built.

Talk about changes in my life. After only six months as the restaurant manager, the regional manager, Cal Fox, announced to the Maine McOpCo market that they were selling all Corporate stores—boom, just like that. As a McOpCo employee, we all had the option of moving to Massachusetts or staying in Maine to work with the operator purchasing your restaurant.

After being promoted in May, I took some time to save up for my next chapter. In October 1986, as I began earning a higher salary and advanced to a managerial position, I made an offer on a condo in Maine, marking my next step towards homeownership.

Steve, my mentor, helped me avoid a big mistake, which became a pivotal moment in my life. He pulled me aside and said, "I can't tell you what to do, but I think you should withdraw your offer on the house." He couldn't tell me why he was against me making a downpayment, but I trusted him. Two weeks later, news broke that McDonald's Corporation was selling all its locations in Maine. Steve thought I'd be one of the people who wanted to move to Massachusetts since they were selling the company-owned stores.

Being so young, I wasn't happy about putting down a $5,000 deposit and risking losing it. Steve foresaw the upcoming changes as we began transitioning the locations to new franchisees at the start of the new year. Consequently, I withdrew my offer without any penalty.

Change is the hardest thing to manage in anybody's life. I was a young kid who grew up in Maine and has only known Maine for my entire life. The culture shift was enormous for me.

I was committed to a long-term relationship with Terry, my girlfriend, but was uncertain how the moving process would affect that. I thought our relationship had a lot of potential and didn't want to give that up. Sure enough, she later became my wife and is a fantastic woman I am lucky to have. We were uncomfortable right from the get-go when we moved to Massachusetts, where significant life changes had presented themselves.

Terry took a leap of faith by moving with me to a new state to start fresh at a new store. We both took a chance on each other as we embarked on this relocation journey together. We officially moved to Massachusetts in January 1987 and rented for 20 months while acclimating to a new state and environment.

It was a hard adjustment for a young couple from Maine. We didn't grow up in a fast-paced environment or a big city like Boston. Suddenly, we were thrown into a world of mayhem in terms of traffic, noise, and amounts of people. People aren't in a hurry where I'm from, so you can imagine the transition.

We were in a familiarly uncomfortable situation - moving and experiencing a new culture shock. Only this time, my wife was pregnant, which was another stressful change. My first daughter was born in Massachusetts in December 1987. In July 1989, my family and I relocated to New Hampshire. It was exciting because we had just bought our first home, and my wife was eight months pregnant with our second daughter.

We considered leaving a year and a half into living in Boston. The adjustment was hard, so we contemplated returning to Maine to work for a McDonald's franchisee. That thought was short-lived because soon after, I was offered a transfer to another store in Lynn, MA. I kept my role and worked there for nearly six years until March 1993.

"Destiny is no matter of chance. It is a matter of choice. It is not a thing to be waited for; it is a thing to be achieved. The torment of precautions often exceeds the dangers to be avoided."
— *Jean de La Fontaine.*

I was promoted from a daily store role to an Area Supervisor on the corporate side, overseeing four to nine restaurant managers. This increased responsibility thrilled me as it allowed me to make a more significant impact on more people.

CHAPTER 3

What Led to the End

"When I talk to leaders, I get the feeling that they are important.
When I talk to leaders, I get the feeling I am important."
— *Alexander Den Heijer*

Part of my professional growth involved further training development. When I became a training consultant from roughly 2011 through 2013, I immediately focused on fine-tuning my presentation skills.

I traveled to Chicago for two weeks to attend a presentation workshop on facilitation skills and leading group discussions. The organizers videotaped everything I did, which immensely helped me improve.

I wholeheartedly recommend this exercise to anyone looking to improve this skill. Being videotaped allowed me to reflect on my performance and ensure I was not starting sentences with incorrect or filler words like "so," "you think," "um," and "ah," among others. It was drilled into us.

It was two weeks focused on:

- Education
- Learning
- Training

- Developing facilitation skills
- Participating
- Properly pronunciating words and speaking, and everything in between!

Instead of incorrectly saying learnin', trainin', or parkin', it's learning, training, and parking. All of this was to become a more effective leader.

The workshop leaders randomly chose a subject to discuss on film and then reviewed the conversation. Through reflection and instruction, we began to work on areas like "non-words" and body language and how they distract or enhance the audience. This event was enjoyable because it was not solely lecture-based but discussion-focused. I was learning leadership styles and skills that would soon prepare me to stand before my crew in the store. I credit my willingness and joy for public speaking to that class. I loved it!

I have witnessed rushed hiring in roles out of urgency, not because they were actively searching for a replacement. They didn't have time or a plan to go through this training. The team didn't attach themselves to the new leader as well or as quickly as they should have been appropriately trained.

I'll always offer people help if they want it. Who knows, maybe I will become a part-time coach, too! There is art in keeping the audience's attention, and it brings me happiness to pass this skill on. While I can't discuss all of the takeaways, one I would like to leave you with is the art of the pause.

As a presenter, facilitator, or even a public speaker, it is essential to emphasize a point by talking clearly and using effective pauses.

For example, your statement may be this:

"We want to exceed our goals by a million dollars."

Then, after making that statement, try to keep quiet and enjoy the silence. While you remain silent, people ponder how they will play their part in exceeding those goals as you emphasize your point. It may seem awkward initially, but it will become second nature with practice.

You have heard me praise McDonald's throughout this book: it is an excellent job with learning opportunities and a rewarding career. I was all-in on my McDonald's career for the longest time and thought I would retire there. All of that changed in November 2001 when the company began mass layoffs.

It was the first time I recall McDonald's evaluating every corporate position for a quality check and validity that the right person was in each role. This included various roles such as field service managers, operations managers, consultants, training consultants, and even senior department heads, covering all leadership positions. From then on, I constantly looked over my shoulder for the last 12 years of my McDonald's career.

At the time, the company had 36 regions, and they were all evaluated at different times for a silent assessment. The evaluator would sit you in the office and discuss your role. My meeting was relatively short, hearing, "You are all set, Charlie. You still have a job. We value you."

Now more than ever, you had to:

- Learn how to and then manage your boss

- Discover what your boss likes and dislikes
- Learn their strengths and weaknesses
- What makes your boss tick and what makes them happy
- Do they want reports ready on their desk when they arrive in the morning?

Unfortunately, not everyone had the opportunity to continue growing with the company and manage their relationship with superiors. These meetings led to two paths: continuing your job in your current role and returning to the office, or being fired and exiting the room while not being allowed to return to the office. I vividly recall the meeting with the Regional Manager and HR Manager, after which several team members I considered friends were asked to leave their roles.

With the implementation of these meetings, you begin questioning everything from each conversation you had with your boss to things you thought you could confide in them when you were having a bad day. Many team members hesitate to confide in their boss, fearing it will be held against them at their subsequent evaluation. Several even went without asking for help due to the fear of a bad performance review.

It was a trying time and, sadly, the beginning of the end for me for a company I loved. I remember telling Greg, "I am always looking over my shoulder, and the culture has changed." Always guarded at work, I learned the importance of accepting and growing.

While contemplating moving on all those years, something never let me leave, so I was forced to trust my instincts and move on. I had said for the longest time, almost ten years before I finally left McDonald's, that I wasn't afraid to go, but I never left. What was the biggest fear?

- Was it the safety and security of my role?
- The paycheck?
- Not succeeding in a new role?
- Not wanting my kids to grow up in a new school, forced to make new friends?
- Or was it left by my colleagues, who I thought I would be in contact with forever?
- I was looking for the ideal job.

You may also be able to relate to this- in life, whether growing up in school, in college, or at a job, you are hyper-focused on that world and the people in it, and you feel you will maintain those relationships forever.

Everyone lives busy lives and goes their separate ways. I have learned that as you go through life if there are two or three people you remain close with, that is a win! It doesn't mean former colleagues don't care about or think about you; you are no longer in their daily lives. The inner voices, or "itty bitty" committee in my head, were challenging me, and it may have been challenging for you, too, at some point.

"When people walk away from you, let them go. Your destiny is never tied to anyone who leaves you, and it doesn't mean they are bad people. It just means that their part in your story is over."
— Julia Roberts

After reflecting, I realized the value I have to offer is not determined by one company assessment. At McDonald's, you can earn countless transferrable skills that can translate into the workplace, including teamwork, leadership, leading teams to improve results, and setting goals and expectations.

Even if you are not in McDonalds, be confident of the tools and skills you have acquired throughout your schooling and work life. Remember, there is a company to which you can add value.

Interestingly enough, before I knew the layoffs were coming in November, I interviewed for a position in the McDonald's Bethesda regional office in Washington for a department head position. I was interviewed by Janet Carson, a lovely lady who gave a strong interview. At this point, I was excited to interview and grow my career in new ways.

She called me the following days of the interview to let me know I didn't get the position. Still, she would have another opportunity available in the next couple of months, and I wouldn't need to interview again if I wanted the job.

She continued to share that after the upcoming company assessments (as I would soon find out, it was a disguising way to say layoffs), she would know more about the availability.

Although I didn't get the position, this call filled me with hope, and then McDonald's announced to the rest of us that they were engaging in layoffs. The company assessed Janet Carson, who interviewed me, and let her go from her position before we could reconnect for the position.

Everything happens for a reason, and although I did not get the job, I love how my life and career turned out. By sharing all this, I challenge you to avoid getting caught up in what I will do with my life afterward. Be aware of what you've learned and how you interacted with the people you met.

Losing out on the President's Awards motivated me and was a turning point in my career. It is an annual award that I secretly always wanted to earn. I strongly felt my contributions over 20+ years were significant enough to win in 2010.

At this point, I was part of the McCafe team in the Boston region. We taught the company how to use the new espresso coffee line for the first time in 2008. By 2010, I ensured the equipment was ordered and delivered on time to start the New Blended Iced Drinks product push.

If something was not working correctly and needed service, I was responsible for deploying help for the entire region. You didn't want to have one store in the state roll out a product if all the other stores could not follow suit.

It was a lot of work, but it was gratifying because I loved the involvement and being able to display proper leadership. I got to know all of the regional franchisees, which helped me in my new jobs that followed.

I wasn't naive to think I would win. So many peers, not just friends, told me, "Charlie, that should have been your award." I knew that, but I also knew that awards aren't the only indicator of success. I performed, and still perform, my job well because I love the roles and serving others.

Due to my heavy emotional investment, I can replay the whole moment of award announcements on March 1, 2011. While nothing is guaranteed, the Boston region typically had one aware winner each year to be recognized from the top 1% of all Global corporate staff.

I felt undervalued and unappreciated, and as you may relate to, being valued in our careers is critical to maintaining fulfillment in the role and success. After losing out on this award in 2010, from that point on, something needed to change. I couldn't be in a position where I'm not growing. Referencing a famous quote from Ray Kroc, the McDonald's Founder. "When you're green, you're growing; when you're ripe, you begin to rot." Ray compares performance to a banana.

Right then and there, I knew that was the sign that I needed to change jobs, and it was my "aha moment." While I had no ill will toward McDonald's and am grateful for everything they have provided in my life, I started to tap into my network to learn if and who else was hiring. This search led me to my role at Antunes and now at Manitowoc Ice. This story should encourage you never to burn a bridge, as you never know when you will work with another party again.

After leaving the McDonald's world, the one thing I did not think of was the impact not changing my phone number would have. After years of dedicated service, I connected with countless people worldwide to effectively lead and perform my job.

If you are in the sales world, if the phone rings, you have to answer. I have found success with clients in sales roles by opening them up to my cell phone line. However, I also had a work phone at H+K for specific customer calls. After I left McDonalds, operators who knew me from my role there kept calling me on my old work number, now my personal phone.

I remember one specific occurrence when I sat with Randy Dutton, my H+K boss, for lunch. We were sitting in a restaurant, and my new work phone rang. Shortly after, I received a work call from a customer on my personal phone, and another call was waiting a minute later. Soon enough, I had three calls going at the same time. It was rather comical. I felt it was unprofessional to have a customer do more work by requesting to call me at a different number than the one they had.

The challenge becomes keeping everybody happy—this balance is an acquired skill I mastered over time. Randy's takeaway from these calls was not a sign of disrespect but that I am busy, successful, and in demand from my customers to solve issues. I have enjoyed all of my roles because I loved being busy. The key is to act as efficiently as possible, something I strive to allow this book to help you do.

While I did move on from McDonald's, a piece of me was missing once I did. Giving back to the community is a huge passion and part of my life. Since I was a young boy, I have learned that I do well serving and helping others.

In my positions at McDonald's, I was also inspired by Ray Kroc's philosophy that we should all take time to give back to our communities.

> *"None of us is as good as all of us."*
> *— Ray Kroc*

During and after working at McDonald's, I was elected and served on the Board of Directors for Ronald McDonald House Charities (RMHCNE) of Eastern New England for ten years, the last four as Vice President. This was my way of "Giving Back." My heart was filled that I was able to impact the lives of many parents and their sick children.

RHMC is separate from McDonald's Corporation and has a 501(c)(3) designation. McDonald's supports RHMC through marketing, donations, and volunteering, among other efforts.

The Kroc family's dedication to philanthropic efforts continued after Ray passed and continues to this day. RHMC proudly celebrated its 50th anniversary, in 2024, as I write this book. His wife, Joan Kroc, donated most of her remaining fortune to different causes for nearly 20 years. Even at the time of her death, $2.7 billion was further distributed to a few organizations.

In the recommended reading section following the final chapter, I suggest a book that delves into this question. Reflect deeply on how to use the money you may never spend wisely.

I would love to share a memorable project I had the privilege of working on. The Manchester, New Hampshire Women's YWCA wanted to offer a room for children to keep themselves occupied while their parents enjoy the facility and receive assistance. Our RMHC charity helped by donating money to remodel a children's room and fill it with toys. In addition to the YWCA, I also hold many memories of working closely with the Big Brothers Big Sisters organization.

In 2019, Ronald McDonald House Charities (RMHC) of Eastern New England and the Ronald McDonald House (RMH) in Providence merged to create Ronald McDonald House Charities New England (RMHCNE). This merger was intended to better serve the needs of children and families in the area.

I was eager to focus on new philanthropic efforts when this merger became official. Three Board of Director groups were now combined, and after ten years, I was eager to impact lives in new ways.

CHAPTER 4

Impact from Dale Carnegie, Ken Blanchard, and Stephen Covey

*"Develop success from failures. Discouragement
and failure are two of the surest
stepping stones to success."*
— *Dale Carnegie*

Three leaders played extraordinary roles in my development, and I will introduce them in the order they entered my life, starting with the crucial lessons I've learned from Dale Carnegie.

I briefly shared how McDonald's allowed me to attend a Dale Carnegie workshop once I was promoted to Assistant Manager and into McOpCo. The company was willing to invest in me to improve my leadership abilities as a manager. I adopted various Carnegie principles and worked towards incorporating them into my life, reinvented as *Charlie's Principles.*

During the first week of the workshop, classes focused on remembering names. Although this wasn't part of the official curriculum, the discussion has stayed with me for over 20 years. There are several key reasons why using names is essential. Here are my favorites to expand from this book's introduction that previewed this chapter:

- It shows appreciation and respect and that you value the interaction.

- Communication becomes more effective as it is more personalized
- It helps build meaningful relationships
- I will provide a few more tips for easy and tangible ways to improve name remembrance:
- Repeat their name in conversation shortly after learning because repetition is one way to reinforce your memory.
- Ask the person to clarify if needed. This is okay because it is not intended to make you feel uncomfortable.
- Write it down, add their contact information to your phone, or connect online.
- Make a connection with the name.

Just recently, while attending a work conference in Vegas for a work trip, I was talking to one of my former bosses from H+K. He came over while I spoke with another colleague; they did not know each other either.

I sensed the awkwardness and quickly made an introduction. Even though they may not have remembered each other's names, this is a sign of common courtesy and respect. It also allows the other person to engage in the conversation if appropriate.

One individual who embodies everything I've discussed is Dave Pickering, a true gentleman. Although our careers have taken us in different directions, we remain friends and catch up occasionally. Dave consistently goes above and beyond to engage in conversations, make appropriate introductions, and ensure everyone is acquainted. He always uses people's names, illustrating the principles of proper introductions I learned in the Dale Carnegie class.

My goal in sharing these stories is to exemplify the importance of doing your best to remember someone's name or, as I advised earlier, re-introducing yourself.

Another Dale Moment

One day of my Dale Carnegie course began with the previous week's assignment: students were to bring in a newspaper of their choosing.

Remember, I was an introvert at this point, and we were tasked with standing in front of 20 people and slamming the newspaper on the desk while making a point in a conversation. I was certainly out of my element. This is one of the turning points in my life that helped me become more outgoing.

The exercise is designed to teach you that you don't need to slam a newspaper down or yell to get the point across. We learned to be assertive and that you don't have to yell, scream, and throw down a newspaper to make your point. The purpose was to get us out of our comfort zones and bring out our different feelings. What it also did for me was help me overcome introversion.

This newspaper analogy hits home in a different way. Some of you reading may be able to relate to not being the biggest fan of your dad. My closest father figure was my Uncle Harold. With my dad being away at sea working for United Fruit Company for six months on and six months off, Harold was someone I could count on for anything. I was always able to talk to him about things I needed a father for:

- Raising kids

- What the best decisions were to make when you are leading a young family
- When I had a challenging day at work

I remember when my dad would just yell at me about how stupid I was. As an introvert, I took the verbal abuse and didn't say a word. Eventually, the emotional pain caused me to get mad and yell back.

My dad thought "slamming a newspaper" would best convey his point. In reality, his style pushed us further apart. There are other ways to communicate more positively. I'm not a yeller; I get that from my mom's side. From how my dad acted, I knew I needed to dig deep to become an extrovert.

During the time my dad was most active in my life, I was at the peak of my introversion. Reflecting, I recall entering a gathering of 10-15 people and quietly standing on the sidelines, shy and reserved. I typically preferred the company of one or two individuals. However, my father's influence eventually altered this aspect of my personality. Despite the occasional negativity in our relationship, this transformation was positive, imparting valuable lessons.

While Dale helped me in those ways, Ken Blanchard impacted me in others. I attended a presentation on "The One Minute Manager" at McDonald's and subsequently read the book. These ideas began to change my life, so I studied him more.

Without Blanchard's thoughts, I would not be the leader I am today. Others unmatch his training principles, and I will share a few of them below.

Ken Blanchard's Training Principles

A. Continuous Feedback: ZAP

Far too often, I see people who don't get any feedback on their jobs. If you want somebody to improve, you must provide them with consistent feedback as frequently as possible. If there is a learning opportunity, it does them more harm to stay silent than help them improve.

What will the outcome be if you tell somebody they need to improve their performance and then say nothing to them for six months? With zero support offered, how can positive change occur? Coaching and insight help others improve, and both need to be present in each employee's tenure at McDonald's or any job.

As a restaurant manager, I provided daily feedback to my shift runners, discussing how their shifts progressed, evaluating their performance, and suggesting areas for improvement.

In this role in the McDonalds world, there are many responsibilities, including:

- Profitability
- Drive-thru service times
- Managing product waste
- Adhering to secondary shelf lives
- Store cleanliness standards
- Labor costs and controls
- Meeting service time standards
- Serving hot food

- Interacting with customers

One of Ken Blanchard's overarching themes was continuous feedback. When you receive a performance review, there should be no surprises.

Book Recommendation: ZAP THE GAPS! Target Higher Performance and Achieve It! - Ken Blanchard, Dana Robinson, and Jim Robinson

This book delves deeper into my earlier statement—you can't just tell someone they need to do better; they must be shown. It helps you identify and correct the factors negatively impacting performance, making the ultimate impact meaningful and measurable.

I have a firsthand story that will help you better understand the Zap Theory, though it was experienced indirectly in this instance.

I spent the day with Bob McDonald, former VP of Operations at McDonald's, and we had a great time. Suddenly, he played his voicemail on speakerphone. If he thought it was a confidential message about me, he wouldn't have done so with me present.

The voicemail was from my current boss: "Bob, I know you're spending the day with Charlie. I don't like how he's handling the Carpenter Organization. He needs to do a better job of putting pressure on them to improve results." At the end of the day, I told Bob I was pleased with how it went, but the voicemail put a damper on an otherwise great day.

At the end of the meeting, I addressed the incident and said, "I had a great day with you, but the voicemail was disheartening."

This was the first I had heard of this issue, and I was both confused and shocked. There was never a single conversation about my performance. I was "Zapped." Questions in my mind became plentiful, including:

- What else was my boss saying about me that he couldn't give feedback personally one-on-one?
- What harm would it have caused if he had?

It diminished my trust in him. A golden rule for a leader is not to tell a superior something without first telling that person. I found this unacceptable because I had never received any constructive feedback or comment about this before it went above my head. This situation is a prime example of making somebody look good by making others look bad. It saddens me to say that this is highly prevalent in the workplace.

B. Setting Incremental Goals ("Chicken in the Box")

When setting goals and trying to achieve them every day, Blanchard refers to the "Chicken in the Box."

Imagine a chicken in a box where the owner places its daily food halfway up. Unaware of its location, the chickens must search for their meal daily. As they wander around, they eventually find the food. Over time, the owner raises the food higher, making it harder to reach, until it's completely out of sight one day. This scenario highlights resilience and adaptability in the face of challenges.

What if the idea of chasing the food revolved around you chasing a goal instead? If you want to achieve a specific food cost or profit goal, you don't know how you will achieve it.

Suddenly, you start working with different ideas to become closer to reaching your goal.

It is nearly impossible for someone to meet all your expectations immediately, so it is essential to communicate them early in someone's training. We need those feel-good situations along the way to help us move forward.

Whether it's feeling good about how your shift went one day and your driving service times the next, you keep moving forward. Once you have achieved your target for driving service times, you can focus on doing better and continuing improvement.

Far too often, bosses expect results too quickly. Remember, Rome wasn't built in a day. The same thing goes for restaurant operations or any job, for that matter. You can lead your time to achieve better times by rewarding them with new expectations, targets, and motivation to get there.

Another impactful leader in my life is Stephen Covey. His philosophies have influenced my job and personal life in countless ways. We can only imagine the innovation, inspiration, and imagination during these chats outside combat.

His book The Seven Habits of Highly Effective People changed my life; it's that simple. All seven habits play a role in my life, and while I won't discuss all seven, I will highlight which habits have had the most significant impact.

The habit I use more than anything is to first "seek to understand, then be understood." Whenever something new comes along, people are afraid to ask questions, and sometimes they're scared to ask the question because they think it's dumb.

I'm never afraid to do that and try to set an example for others. During my presentations at McDonald's, I always said it in black and white: "There are no dumb or silly questions." I also provided templates for them during my talks. One being,

"Hey, I'm just asking this question to seek an understanding of what you're trying to convey." These questions also help the person leading the presentation, as they may need to clarify a point.

In my presentations, if I sense the audience isn't fully engaged, I might pose a question to which I already know the answer. This approach encourages those hesitant to speak up, fostering a more open dialogue. The response often generates more questions and leads to a more robust, in-depth conversation about a crucial point I was trying to convey.

It is fulfilling when people say to me, "Thank you very much for breaking the ice," or "Thank you for asking that question because I didn't want to ask it." The other habit that immediately comes to mind is "Win-Win."

I was in Malaysia in 2023 and visited the McDonald's equipment team. The equipment manager continuously criticized Manitowoc Ice, claiming their performance has declined over the past five years. However, all these issues predated my tenure with the company.

Have you ever been in a situation where someone says the same thing three, four, or five times, thinking repetition gets it a point further? Eventually, as I became frustrated but remained calm, I finally said, "I understand what you are saying about how we have messed up. I can't do anything about the past, but we can move forward together in the future to make this right. Let's make it a win-win for everybody. You have gotten your point forward. Let's learn from this.:

How I handled it diffused the situation and rebuilt a positive relationship for our brand. Ever since this conversation, things have gone smoothly and exceptionally. Move past the little things and focus on the present.

My third most impactful habit is self-explanatory, "Being Proactive." If tasks or events that you know need to be changed in an organization or are unique are coming up, we must anticipate that better results will not be achieved in one week. As leaders, we need to understand how changes benefit the company.

The next habit I will dive into is "Beginning with the End in mind," painting the picture of what success looks like.

Far too many people think of the immediate tasks without a plan, which can seem daunting. Reaching the end goal is a process that requires a plan to come to fruition. Painting the long-term vision helps people understand the process of getting there. Know where you're going, find small ways to get there, and focus on that goal. It is easy to become overwhelmed if you solely focus on the end goal rather than how you will arrive at the destination.

Unrealistic goals were set, or they weren't SMART goals:

- **S**pecific
- **M**easurable

- **A**chievable/ Actionable/ Attainable
- **R**elevant
- **T**ime-Bound

Is the time I allow my employees to achieve this goal realistic, or am I setting them up for failure, a mental breakdown, and added stress? It may seem common sense as you read, but leadership often and incorrectly places unrealistic expectations on their workforce. You may be able to relate to this at some point in your life: Management expects too much.

Often, simple tasks need to be corrected, which can help them move forward. As a leader, are you easily accessible and approachable to your employees? Help your team adopt the mindset, "Let's complete the task in the process first and then focus on task two."

Ray Kroc, whose quote I mentioned earlier, always emphasized continual self-improvement and growth. As the founder, he is one of the key individuals who helped turn McDonald's into a global powerhouse brand. Ray purchased the rights to McDonald's franchise from the McDonald brothers, Dick and Mac.

Interestingly enough, Ray feels that McDonald's began when his store opened in Des Plaines, Illinois, in 1955, rather than when the brothers launched in 1940.

His dedication to building McDonald's into a successful brand was so strong that he mortgaged his home, risking its loss, to make timely franchising payments. He needed liquidity to achieve his goal of traveling and boosting brand awareness.

It can also be considered similar to sharpening the saw, a reference to Steven Covey. As a leader, you must do everything possible to prevent rotting and maintain a sharp saw or fine-tune your skills.

One way to prevent the "banana from rotting" is to improve performance constantly. General statements should be avoided in performance reviews because they don't help anyone improve. When discussing performance, you must also be careful when using personality statements.

If I told you, "Vince, I don't like your attitude." Attitude means something different to everyone and is too broad and a gray-based statement to be on a performance review.

How do they improve on that "attitude problem" with no backing? The employee is left wondering,

- "Is it that I'm too short with my answers?"
- "Do I yell too much?"

As I matured as a leader, I could easily pick who did not have their head in the game during their shifts. Often jumpy and defensive, I hear this:

"Well, what exactly doesn't look good?"

Think more like, How can we make this response constructive?

Specific feedback would include:

- While I appreciate you arriving to work on time, your hair's not combed. It may help you remember if you leave a comb by your car keys.

- Although your uniform could be more orderly, you did great at the fry station. A tip that used to work for me is checking my uniform for appearance when I leave my car for work.
- You always give your best effort each shift. You were late for work. Something that may work for you is leaving 15 minutes earlier than you usually do.

Providing specific feedback became a game-changer in helping others grow as I learned not to use the words "but" or "however" when providing it. This all sounds basic, but it is highly overlooked and essential. Like this knowledge, much of the wisdom I learned from Carnegie, Blanchard, and Covey multiplied with the more responsibility I received. Instead of focusing on one store's staff and profitability, I was promoted to Area Supervisor and oversaw nine stores. The increased responsibility excited me because I was able to make a more significant impact on more people.

As a manager, my daily feedback was to my shift managers and assistant managers. I then transitioned to providing input to several restaurant managers on how they run their restaurants daily from an operations perspective. This would involve ongoing communication to monitor the month's goals and objectives.

As I joined Manitowoc Ice in 2022, the feelings of a new job were excitement, nervousness, and optimism. After my first performance with my boss after I joined, one of the most positive people I know, Greg Ebel, my current boss, said during my first performance review, "You're never going to hear anything that we haven't previously discussed." This statement became a memorable conversation about Ken Blanchard, and he turned out to be correct. The performance reviews were a recap of things they had already said. We also discussed Ken Blanchard's teachings and principles and how we applied them to our careers.

The One Minute Praise immediately comes to mind when I think of Greg. He was exceptional at implementing this concept from Ken Blanchard. Greg has created an atmosphere of openness and fostered a great, trusting environment. His ability to actively listen, show respect for ideas, and always be willing to hear what you say about a potential solution separates him as an incredible leader.

I was recently reflecting on my McDonald's career with a friend, and he asked if I had any memories of Greg's praise or pump-up speeches that he had given at one point.

My answer was *every* time I talked to him. He dove into problems that surfaced and was fearless in facing challenges head-on.

I learned a lot from him and applied his teachings when he hired me as a global manager. Greg hired me to take care of problems and challenges in the store for the McDonald's account so he could focus on the rest of his job and broader responsibilities. As he challenged me, he always provided me with a takeaway. There was a regular feedback loop for me to improve because correction action is impossible without feedback.

To prepare for year-end 2023, I needed to catch up on getting everything done beforehand to prepare for our McDonald's annual business review. It was my first time going through it, and I struggled to assemble everything. He came in asking why I wasn't done yet but pushed me in a way that wasn't negative push, but friendly.

He said, "I'm sorry I had to come down on you."

While I appreciated his apology, I didn't feel it was necessary. Greg expects a lot from you and wants you to succeed in life. The way he provides feedback helps foster accountability and enables others to improve and act on it instead of putting you down.

Bo Erickson, Greg's superior, leads by example and acts in a way that he'd like to see everybody act. I can describe him as a personable, welcoming guy with a solid human connection. He is very proactive in communication and strives for and demands positive results.

He has a good way of speaking and encourages others to participate in open conversations. You've probably seen and heard people, the yellers and screamers, pounding their fists: "WE'VE GOT TO MEET OUR GOALS!" whether you've got the yellows or the screamers.

The above quote is the opposite of Bo. He is a boss you would want to work for because of his mannerisms and behaviors. He cares about the people under him becoming successful at their jobs and seamlessly creates that environment. With that, Bo also cared deeply about creating a winning environment built on trust, where people want to show up.

Picture here is Greg Ebel and his boss, Bo Erickson. They have entrusted me as Vice President- McDonald's Global account. They do not micromanage me, they respect my decisions and support me 100%

CHAPTER 5

Mentors Throughout My Career

The delicate balance of mentoring someone is not creating them in your own image but giving them the opportunity to create themselves
— Steven Speilberg

I am eternally grateful for my mentors, and it's crucial to leverage yours to your advantage, as they can provide invaluable guidance. As you've read, my book mentions Steve Walach in several places. Several other mentors helped me get to where I am today. When I look back at when I became a store manager, Glenn Ivy became a mentor figure to me.

We were within five miles of each other at different stores, being a peer we could all count on if needed. As a young manager, the experience he had already been through provided me with clarity, guidance, and advice. A conversation with Glenn helped me realize that while many of us have mentor figures in our lives, some may not know just how large of an impact they have made.

When I was promoted to assistant manager in Portland, Maine, Glenn was my store manager when I became an assistant. He moved down from Northern Maine to take a position in this particular restaurant in Portland. As we were both newly acclimating to this store, we had common ground and forged an excellent professional relationship to this day.

Once I was promoted to store manager, he became my tutor. He coached me on how to succeed and maintain a strong company culture. By then, he had become more than just a tutor and colleague; he was also a friend. Now, he remains a cherished friend.

While in Las Vegas in July 2024, attending a McDonald's licensee conference, I caught up with an old counterpart in the McDonald's world, Todd Arnold. We just had a back-and-forth, and the conversation that came up was about people who have impacted our lives. I shared a Steve Walach story, and he shared a story about Henry Gonzales, a Former East Division President of McDonald's. I also saw Steve Walach at a meeting two weeks later in Boston. I shared that I am writing a book, and he is a part of it. I'm unsure if he realized the extent of his role in my life, but I hope this book will help him know how appreciated he is.

One of my respected colleagues came from the sales arena. Susan was a manager at McDonald's who left to work for Blockbuster Video in the 1990s. We all know what happened to that chain: it went under. As excited as she was for the next chapter, her transition was challenging.

When working at McDonald's, you are involved in a fast-paced job, always on the go and always thinking. While you are still connecting with customers working in a job like CVS, a grocery store, or Blockbuster, it is an environment opposite to McDonald's. There is nothing wrong with that; for some people, this environment is preferred, but from my perspective, the only thing I see when I walk into a store like CVS is the assistant manager stocking shelves, which is night and day from working at McDonald's. In one world, you are juggling several tasks and adapting to new deadlines, which can be exhilarating and tiring. In the other world, there is much more time for reflection, but in comparison, it is at a snail's pace and with dying technology.

Eventually, Susan returned to McDonald's. Through the grapevine, I learned she decided to return because of my impact on her. This was heartwarming in many ways, but knowing I made just as big of an effect on her as she did on me is a treasured memory.

> *There's an employee out there who still thinks of*
> *you because you were kind to them.....*
> *Never stop being that leader.*
> *— Jessica Luna*

All of us have that one person that influenced our career. Have you communicated that to anybody? I suggest you be upfront and honest with a particular boss or leader you admire or idolize and let them know how they motivated you.

Equally as impactful on me was John Lacus, a man I have known for 30+ years. I first met John during my days as an area supervisor. A Burger King restaurant in Middleton, Massachusetts, closed because of bankruptcy, and McDonald's purchased the rights to the land and building. Somehow, we converted it into a McDonald's restaurant in 30 days, something scarce in the food service world, although it was difficult.

When I first entered the store, although closed, it was still a Burger King. I needed help understanding this system, which was like a foreign language. I saw different equipment than we used at the Golden Arches, including a "bag-in-box soda system," which I had never seen.

It came down to thinking about what we needed. I called Coca-Cola for assistance, and John Lucas walked in the next day. He helped me convert the soda systems that McDonald's required and made a stressful situation seem easy. I was thankful he took care of everything that was needed.

I noticed him at different work-related events over the years. I ran into John at many trade shows throughout my career. When I joined the supplier ranks a few years later, I would still see John and say hello. We became closer as the years progressed.

I always worked hard to pick his brain. As a very strong-willed sales expert, he was always open to giving sound advice. You could tell by his mannerisms that he loved his job.

His career led him to a company called Welbilt, and when I worked for Antunes, our paths continued to cross at different meetings. I always looked up to him, and I am unsure if he realized quite the impact he made on me.

When I first had that job at Antunes, I was no longer focused on McDonald's. I was focused on water filtration. He was the guy I would always talk to you about areas like, "What did you do in this situation?", "What did you do over here?", "How did you do this?" I wanted to learn from him and always asked him questions.

He taught me and reinforced the importance of communicating with the operators and the follow-up. His strength was building relationships, and coming from McDonald's, I knew the value of that skill set. Your number one responsibility is building and maintaining relationships and building trust. After leaving Antunes, I went to work for H+K next.

I was now selling all kinds of equipment to McDonald's as a Kitchen Equipment Supplier (KES):

- Grills
- Fryers
- Spatulas and other small wares
- Soda systems
- Shake machines, and the list goes on.

John helped me understand the Welbilt brand's product line. If you ever Google "Welbilt Brands," you will see that they own Frymaster (fryers), Manitowoc Ice (ice machines), Garland (grills), and Kolpak (exterior boxes).

He took the time to train me on all the lines he represented because I was selling his product to McDonald's. After spending

time with John, I felt more comfortable about the equipment choices the operators had to choose from.

When I met with operators to see if they were interested in more effective ice machines, there were two brands to choose from. They didn't want anyone depending on one particular vendor to supply each needed area. Since vendors don't have specified contract length guarantees, they are relentlessly working to keep McDonald's happy. For example:

- <u>Ice Machines:</u> Manitowoc and Scotsman
- <u>Grills:</u> Garland and Taylor
- <u>Fryers:</u> Frymaster and Henny Penny
- <u>Exterior Cooler/Freezer Boxes:</u> Kolpak and Norlake

John ensured he trained me on all Welbilt brands so I could better understand them and sell more effectively. I emulate what I learned from John and spend time with the different markets.

In 2024, I worked for Manitowoc Ice, selling ice machines. Manitowoc Ice was acquired by Pentair in 2022 and previously sold by Welbilt. In John's case, several companies were underneath their brand, so he sold all of those brands through H+K and Franke.

Pictured here is John Lacus and myself. I credit John with teaching me everything I've learned in the "Sales" arena. He is fearless, listens well and has a way about himself. I have considered him my life Mentor in all of the positions I've held.

CHAPTER 6

More Managerial Lessons: Conflict Resolution, Constructive Feedback and Communication, Overworking Your Team, The Power of "But"

"Leaders do not avoid, repress, or deny conflict, but rather see it as an opportunity."
— *Warren Bennis*

Improving Conflict Resolution

When I started at McDonald's, Eddy, the store manager, pulled me aside and called me out for something no one else dared to say: "Charlie, my god, you've got bad breath!"

Often, people will not say anything because it can seem awkward or uncomfortable. By asking the difficult question, you are helping the other person. It may be embarrassing for a short moment, but you have helped them take action to remedy the issue. This was my first memory of handling an uncomfortable conversation working at McDonald's. In this case, I was the recipient. Indeed, I was embarrassed, but I thanked him for bringing this to my attention. It seemed like a tiny issue, but Eddy demonstrated how easy it was to handle a delicate situation.

Once you have practiced with these conversations, it becomes easier when a situation comes up. I had this conversation with several employees later in my career about body odor.

It was our fault nine out of ten times because we didn't provide multiple uniforms to employees. Who has time to wash clothes if they are working the next day or three days in a row? There were few, and I discovered this problem because many staff members worked 40+ hours weekly.

My lesson learned, and takeaway is to continually challenge others to ask questions. Eddy wasn't mad but embarrassed and appreciative; I didn't let it go unnoticed. By me being honest, things changed for the better.

For years after this, in all levels of my job, it became easier for me to have those difficult conversations, and not about body odor or bad breath, but with very sensitive issues while dealing with cases of sexual harassment, misreporting of food cost, and several HR or performance related issues. Although my issue of bad breath is very minute, any time I am dealing with a problematic situation, I always think of that first time I was told, "I have bad breath."

Strong conflict resolution skills are essential to creating and maintaining a healthy work environment, but they're only one piece of the puzzle. After addressing these conflicts, as leaders, we next need to provide constructive feedback to ensure that everyone can learn from each situation and grow. When we shift from correcting an issue to offering honest feedback, we help prevent similar problems from arising again.

Failure to address conflict may lead to:

- Resentment,
- Poor teamwork,
- Lack of communication, and, although maybe indirectly,
- Condoning the conflict.

Finding ways to handle our internal conflict to be the ultimate team player is not easy but necessary. We all go through those challenging days and keeping it all in is unhealthy. Eventually, if you do, you're in your head in a harmful way. You must move forward and remember there will always be good and bad days. Be here now. Be present. Be in the moment.

"Don't let circumstances affect responsibility." Excuses for missing goals or being late won't change accountability for your results. I learned this from NFL Coach Bill Belichick. Belichick was still furious when a player was late due to a snowstorm. He believes in holding everyone accountable, regardless of adversity. We are all human, and it's extremely easy to be distracted. I tell my managers when needed if I appear slightly distracted.

- Your wife or husband is sick.
- Your child is sick.
- You are sick.

No matter the external factors, we must focus on the job and the situation. Communication is key when something comes up. Communicate with your team, stay busy, and mitigate the distraction. I have a long-time phrase that applies to this situation professionally. "Fake it until you make it" regarding customer interaction.

One of the foundational elements of service-based business is not to let outside problems affect your working shift. If you're having a bad day before your shift, it is crucial to curb the challenges and take your mind off the issues. It is essential to recognize the moments we are in.

For example, if you're a shift manager with some challenges at home that carry over to your shift, it can negatively impact the entire crew working underneath you. Here is the golden lesson: never take your frustration out on others.

As a leader, I want to show empathy for my team during hard times but also encourage two areas:

1. A positive experience with a customer may be the reason they come back again, and a smile can make all the difference in someone else's bad day.
2. Work can serve as an outlet or coping mechanism.

Whether you are behind on rent payments, your car broke down, or you had a death in the family, staying busy can help ease the pain. When my mom passed in January 2024, I used work to help me cope with it.

Consider this scenario: You are only allocated three sick days per year at work. If you fall ill again or face another situation, you will have exhausted your three sick days.

There are a few ways of thinking to approach this:

- "This shift is going to be terrible tonight."
- "I am going to quit and figure out the next step."
- "I am going to make the most of this shift and rest when I get home."

Say you're a manager; three people call out of a shift. As leaders, we must set the tone and immediately calm that situation. As leaders, it is vital to not:

- Make any rash decisions in the area of change.
- Panic

It's still a glass of milk on the kitchen floor. Oh my god, I can't believe it!

Sometimes, that's when people have had the "last straw" on a bad day. Similar to my mom, she was always very calm. Another way I can describe her is having impeccable humor. She relieves tension in others by adding a twist of humor to help the situation heal.

Providing constructive feedback to a new hire

Feedback often ties into conflict resolution. The difference between providing constructive input and complaining without action can drastically affect a company's overall health and success.

When leaders focus on feedback, they can create an environment that encourages employees to feel confident, empowered, heard, and valued. This, in turn, allows leaders to help employees tap into their full potential.

I remember one time when I interviewed this young lady. At 16, Rachel seemed like a go-getter, very gracious, and had an infectious smile. I immediately thought she'd be a superstar so I hired her.

This hire was my last task before leaving for a vacation. When I returned home, I was eager to learn how Rachel had been doing. A fellow manager, Linda, described her performance as awful and said she was doing poorly. I was shocked by these remarks, so I asked what she had done wrong.

"She is barely talking to customers."

"She is not keeping herself busy."

"She hasn't been very friendly."

Although shocked by our manager's statements, my next question was, when did you bring this to Rachel? Sure enough, I learned no feedback was given, yet she still felt comfortable speaking negatively about this employee.

Let's put ourselves in Rachel's shoes: trying to stay calm and confident in a first job.

At sixteen, the idea of a paycheck, independence, and a step toward adulthood excited her. Now, standing at the threshold, nerves and doubts began to creep in as there was no support around her. With no support, trying to calm the butterflies in her stomach was an overwhelming task.

How can an employee succeed without direction, coaching, or mentorship? The three of us sat down, and I told Rachel, "I hired you for your smile."

"We want to provide you with feedback to improve each day. I want you to feel positive and feel good about working here."

Once I shared certain things we'd like to see her do better, she immediately became the superstar I had hoped she would be.

It doesn't matter if you are a new manager, crew member, group leader, or manufacturing plant manager: you need to know and understand the expectations of your role. More importantly, you need to be set up for success. As leaders, it is our job to set everyone else up for success.

If others don't know your expectations, they will likely flounder. You set them up for failure into this success when they don't know what to expect.

While providing constructive feedback is essential, how we deliver it is equally important. The way we give feedback can make a significant difference. An overly common drawback in providing feedback is using the word "but." While it might seem harmless, it is not.

The Power of "But" and "However" - Charlie's Principle

The word "but" frequently sneaks into conversations. It often signals an impending critique cloaked in a seemingly positive remark.

Consider how often you hear someone say, "I like how you handled that customer, but... you need to work on your appearance."

- "...you need to speak slower."
- "... you did this and that wrong."

At first, the compliment feels genuine, but the moment "but" appears, the anticipation of criticism overshadows any warm statements or praise. The word "but" acts as a spotlight, highlighting flaws and dimming the glow of positive feedback.

This pattern happens so often that the initial compliment fades into the background, and we brace ourselves for the inevitable negative comment.

I advise eliminating the "but" word. Try it yourself and let me know what you find.

I remember a performance review with my old boss at H+K, Randy Dutton. Every successful or positive comment he wrote was followed by "but" or "however."

Here's an example of an incorrect use of the word "but": "Charlie, you have done a fantastic job this past year. You have achieved sales of 5M, BUT we still have a high amount of excessive inventory we need to sell..."

I was very irritated by continuously ruined positive moments. There must have been over ten positive comments followed by "but" or "however." Understanding this subtle yet powerful word can help us communicate more effectively. It also allows us to appreciate compliments without the looming shadow of criticism genuinely. A leadership standard is to "Praise in Public," and "Criticize in Private."

Now that you understand the impact of language, including the word "but," it is crucial to know how to motivate and communicate with others. Using an incorrect word can undermine what was meant to be thoughtful and constructive feedback, and pushing too hard in the workplace can lead to similar unintended outcomes.

I want to highlight another area of Randy's impact: He gave me the confidence to stop looking over my shoulder at work.

I struggled to be myself once McDonald's introduced assessments and began undermining management. Randy helped fix my temporary mindset shift and helped me carve my future without hesitation.

The Lesson of Overworking an Assistant Manager

There was a time when I had a superb assistant manager working under me, Cheryl. This role required 46 to 50 hours a week, and I overburdened her in my eagerness to excel. Eventually, she handed in her notice, and I was deeply saddened, knowing that my actions had driven her to quit. The demanding hours were a central talking point for her during her exit interview.

Steve Walach could have quickly criticized me for this mistake. Others might have pointed out my error, saying, "Look what you did; you caused her to quit." I have learned to admit when you make a mistake, as it will help you move forward faster.

He chose a different approach, and I am thankful he did. His response taught me a crucial lesson about leadership and life. Steve understood I was already remorseful, and additional rebuke wouldn't help.

Sometimes, you must accept the consequences of your actions, and the situations life throws at you. While you can't change the past, you can face it with a mindset geared toward learning from the situation. Instead of harsh criticism, he offered me the space to reflect and grow from my error. This experience has shaped my perspective on handling similar situations in the future.

Leadership Lessons Part 2

Work-Life Balance Challenges, An Example of
Poor Leadership, First Impressions

"I am not afraid of an army of lions led
by a sheep; I am afraid of an army of sheep
led by a lion."
— Alexander the Great

Work-Life Balance Challenges

Have you ever responded to an email in the middle of the night? Did it end up sounding better or worse than you intended? Or does replying when well-rested lead to clearer communication?

A leader's actions may set incorrect expectations for the rest of their team, regardless if those expectations are not explicitly stated. For example, if a leader regularly shows up late for work, team members will likely begin doing the same. In a different example, if a boss consistently answers emails during the hours most are resting for the next day, it may unintentionally and sublimely signal to lower-level employees and subordinates that they should also be available and responsive during off-hours. In other words, your staff should always be working.

This behavior may create a poor cultural norm. Employees model the behavior of their leaders. Over time, if employees are up checking their phones all night, it may lead to potential burnout and limited work-life balance. If someone misses one of these late emails, unspoken pressure may build.

To take it a step further, they may develop the fear of missing out, or FOMO, about important messages. The central theme of sharing this is if perceived expectations are built incorrectly, adverse workplace effects will follow. As a leader, your employees will follow your example, whether it leads to positive or negative outcomes.

With these feelings of being overwhelmed, it is easy to react impulsively, not just by answering emails when overtired. When it is not the right time or place to respond to a situation, and for whatever reason, we may react unintentionally. It is essential to recognize how we are feeling and what is causing these emotions:

- Traffic
- Fight with a significant other
- Financial constraints

Many years ago, a team member was doing her job, which was stirring hotcake mix. Out of nowhere, she became outraged and slammed the batter. Picture liquid and raw batter slowly finding new homes on the walls and floors.

The initial reaction of many managers, not leaders, would have been to send her home or make a snap decision to fire her. By reacting negatively, we don't help the person. Did they just have an emotional moment? Is there something else going on outside of the workplace? They may just need a moment to take a deep breath, walk, and gather their thoughts.

Once she cooled down, she apologized and helped clean up the mess after a few minutes. Again, firing them does nothing but set them up for a further downward spiral. In this particular case, the "real" story was her mom had been ill at home, unable to work, and money was tight. The fiasco with the hotcake batter was triggered by something that had nothing to do with work but rather her deepening concerns with her mom. You can draw from this story, as it's important to remember that we often don't know what occurs outside of work. I've learned that some situations require a compassionate approach rather than a reprimand.

This person had a learning opportunity to grow, not make their day worse. I hope this story inspires you to go above and beyond to help your team identify the problem before rushing decisions. While this is easier said than done, work to recognize emotions in heated moments before reacting poorly.

If the pressure is always on due to around-the-clock responsibilities, employees will need a place to outlet their stress. In the McDonald's world, an easy method to manage stress and anxiety is stress eating. It may sound obvious, but it is worth stating that our well-being can be affected by work habits and actions.

On a shift, the quickest way to have a meal is to have a quick sandwich on your break. Over time, these sandwiches, fries, and desserts add up against your health. My book focuses on recognizing the training and the recognition of what it is. I felt called to share improvements on how to get better in life: I was up to 290 pounds before finally getting back down to 209 pounds (the weight on my driver's license!).

Put yourself in my shoes, surrounded by McDonald's fresh French fries all day; the temptation was real! In all fields, but especially in the fast-food world, it is essential to be mindful of how you consume your daily nutrition. To begin taking better care of my health, I started packing a healthy lunch daily to ensure I was not consuming our food three meals per day. I'd like to mention that it's okay to eat McDonald's food occasionally.

Many of these challenges can be avoided by leaders *being leaders*. When we lead by example and set good habits for our team, not only does company culture improve, but so does the well-being of our team. We can take actions, including only responding to emails during the workday or explicitly stating that after-hours responses are not expected, encouraging consuming a diet focused on moderated daily fast food, and encouraging a solid work-life balance.

An Example of Poor Leadership

In preparation for writing this book, I compiled a list of all the bosses I remembered from my time at McDonald's and reflected on those who didn't perform as well.

This was the first story that came to mind as a restaurant manager when I was involved in an intense, closely monitored relationship. It seemed that almost every day or every other day,

I would hear in a bombarding and demeaning way, "What are you doing today to make your store better? What are you doing? What's your plan?" to get me to spend my time on short-term tasks.

> *"Be thankful for all the difficult people in your life, and learn from them. They have shown you exactly who you do not want to be."*
> — *Unknown*

Reflecting, I know he wanted what was best for the store with good intentions. I say this with good intentions, but continuously questioning tactics and micromanaging led to an unmotivating role. In this environment, I never felt valued.

The supervisor at the time didn't care about me as a person. It was a classic "just another number employee" situation, and it was displayed in their actions toward the staff. Nothing was ever good enough, and I lacked self-worth and accomplishment.

I remember bringing up a staffing issue and being immediately dismissed. The counter I received was, "What are you doing today to make tomorrow better?" While that is necessary at certain times, it doesn't have a long-term vision built into the smaller tasks.

Whether you want to fix a staffing issue, improve service time, or reduce food costs, you don't do it in one day. You accomplish it over time.

Long-term goals are more critical in situations because they focus on continuous improvement daily and weekly. Slight improvement over time will eventually allow us to hit six-month and year-long goals.

He was only worried about today, which is of utmost importance, but with little regard for how his actions today impacted tomorrow. For my entire tenure under him, I felt like I had a hand or a thumb on top of me and vowed never to be like that as I climbed the company ladder. A big takeaway is that when micromanaging is present, it is a missed opportunity to improve the culture and overall team growth.

I remember when he called me to say he had been offered a promotion. To this day, I can vividly remember holding the phone and pumping my fist. I was ecstatic because a promotion for him meant I would report to someone else as a new boss!

First Impressions with Andy Wilson and Lisa

First impressions can significantly impact our perception and overall satisfaction. Andy Wilson embodied that better than anyone else I have known. I worked under him before becoming a Store Manager.

I'll never forget his name because of the lessons he shared. When I was a new shift manager, Andy always provided feedback. One critical conversation stood out to me as a vital learning moment, and I have replicated it several times throughout my career as I trained new managers.

He brought me out from behind the counter to stand in the lobby to discuss what I observed in the store, which is a big deal at McDonald's, but you may have yet to learn if you have never been to it.

"Charlie, tell me what you see?" I relished the opportunity and discussed the organization of the front counter and center island, how the crew engaged with each other, and everything in between!

Returning to view your workplace from the customer's perspective is invaluable. It allows you to see the environment and service through their eyes, helping you identify areas for improvement and opportunities to enhance their experience.

Imagine walking through a store's doors for the very first time. What are the first things you notice?

- Is it welcoming?
- Clean?
- Does the staff seem approachable?

I call moments like this "learning by example." They put you in the customer's shoes and analyze areas that can be improved. Andy Wilson taught me to do this; I could do it for countless others. Now, he also passes the lesson on to you in this book.

It all comes down to those we are impacted by and who we impact in our careers. Like Andy, Lisa did the same for me when I was in school and working at the South Portland location as a closing manager under her as my superior. She firmly believed in me and pushed me hard to make me a better manager.

I worked late Friday night until midnight and could not wait to get home to rest finally. It was one of those shifts that required all of my energy. After tossing and turning in bed, I finally fell asleep, but I woke to her phone call at 5 a.m.

"Hello?"

"Get your a** into the store now."

To say she chewed me out would be an understatement. "...just get back to the store right now and fix the condition you left it in." These words left an impression on me still until today.

After this experience, my way of doing things changed for the better. For the rest of my career, every time I worked as a closing manager, even as an assistant manager, closing at night, I would never forget that phone call that Saturday morning. It shaped me for the better. She continued to share with Steve how well I was doing. Despite this incident, I had an excellent track record and reputation with the company, proving that I learned a lesson from it.

Being on the other side of the counter with Andy brought me back to six years prior when I was the shift manager in Westbrook, Maine. When he came into the store, he called me out for the way the store looked. He highlighted my initial weakness in maintaining cleanliness standards.

It was an eye-opener experience, and I knew he was right. Wisdom is acquired after experience when you can sit back and reflect. Often, though not intentionally, your focus may be on the wrong priority for that moment when you're in the middle of all of your responsibilities as an in-store manager.

When you do the same things every day, and new habits become old, you can mistakenly wear blinders. Andy changed my mindset and helped me "not get caught with your pants down" again throughout my career.

To be honest, I needed to get a good kick in the butt to get a keen eye towards getting a cleaner restaurant. This experience led me to implement weekly cleaning programs and manager accountability underneath me.

I held my managers and other management team members accountable for specific areas of the restaurant, which is very common in the food service industry. We had different managers responsible for various store areas following my direction.

A strong wake-up call can send you in two directions: motivated or ready to give up. Always view a situation as an opportunity to learn and grow. This moment propelled my career advancement and beyond.

CHAPTER 8

More Value from Stories of My Past

"The past is behind, learn from it.
The future is ahead; prepare for it.
"The present is here; live it."
—Thomas S. Monson

Augusta, ME Incident with Napkins

In the first few years after the millennium, I was working a field service job that required me to visit various restaurants in the area. One of my stops was at the drive-thru in Augusta, ME.

I had a great visit.

The food and fries were quality.

There was excellent speed of service.

The store looked tidy and orderly.

After eating, I shared these remarks with the manager, along with the only area for improvement I noticed, "I was given about 15 napkins with my one order." Although I meant it to be both a learning and profit opportunity for them, the takeaways from them were not what I intended them to be.

Rather than focusing on how nearly everything was exceptional, giving too many napkins overpowered the rest of the experience. In the grand scheme, it was meant as such a minuscule opportunity. It took away from the actual message: I had a great visit and kicked myself with that because that was their takeaway. The focus must remain on the customer, and providing adequate utensils or napkins is just one part of their total experience.

> *You can tell a bully from a leader by how they*
> *treat people who disagree with them.*
> *— Miles K. Davis*

It can be easy to allow one minor setback to overshadow a situation's positive aspects, but any hiccups are just a tiny part of the bigger picture. When we keep a balanced view, we can navigate challenges with a more positive outlook.

I challenge you to remember that everything has its ups and downs. Do your best to keep one area of struggle from making you forget any progress. While we embrace the good, we must also learn from the bad and keep improving.

Conversations about Leaving Nursing

At one point a few years ago, my daughter Brianna, shared that she was thinking about leaving nursing and going into accounting. She is good at math and confident in her abilities, coupled with her business acumen—I'd like to say she got some of that from me! We had an open conversation, and while she has those skill sets, she is very talented at what she does. I wanted to help her try to identify her true self.

I provided her with several pieces of advice as she continued to self-reflect after our talk:

1. Imagine different scenarios in both and see how each makes you feel
2. Write down your actual long-term goals
3. Weigh the pros and cons of each
4. Trust your gut — go with your intuition.
5. You have an amazing heart and a nurturing way about yourself.

She opted to stay in a nursing and is now at a "Supervisor" level. I am one proud dad.

My Daughter's Job at Circle K — Teaching By Actions —

Like her grandmother, my oldest daughter, Sarah, is very methodical and keeps her thoughts to herself. If I make one point on a subject and my wife makes another, she always takes a neutral "Switzerland," position. One day, we were discussing training your people at work. She felt that she did not do well in this area, and I asked why she felt that way.

She responded that she is very reserved. I gave her a tip that people often learn and react from body language, not just words. I've had plenty of folks who worked for me in the past where I realized just because they're not talking doesn't mean they don't communicate. Regardless of how you do it, your team needs to know what to do in all situations, not just the easygoing days. Leadership by example is a must.

She shared a story about how a soda machine went down in one of her stores. Her assistant manager freaked out and immediately began panicking. Sarah told her to call the service department to get it fixed and not to worry.

"Sarah, how can you be so calm about it?"

"What else can we do," she replied.

Sarah continued, "It's just soda. All you can do is what you can do. We are not soda fountain service providers. You can't control what happened."

I was so proud of her for recognizing the gravity of the situation. She was training through her actions, and her calm leadership profoundly impacted the employee's development.

Here's another training lesson:

Another instance was when one of her young cashiers had an irate customer who didn't want to sell her alcohol. After all, she felt she was buying the alcohol for a minor. This customer decided to try another location. The message that got back to my daughter was that the cashier on duty gave the phone number to the operations manager.

As it turned out, the employee did not give out the phone number, which is another example of the importance of communication. We must teach our teams not to give out private personal phone numbers without consent and the system in place if this occurs.

Pictured above are my two daughters, Brianna (left), Sarah (right). As a parent, one can only hope that have learned something from her mom and I. We can lead them to the water, but they need to drink the water on their own. We are so proud of them, as any parent would be of their children.

The Importance of Body Language in Leadership

I found an impactful article from Forbes on five ways body language affects leadership. It can help you immediately take action to improve your leadership effectiveness:

1. You make an impression in less than seven seconds
2. Building trust depends on your verbal-nonverbal alignment
3. Focus on what you say when you talk with your hands

4. Your most influential communication medium is (still) face-to-face
5. If you can't read body language, you are missing half the conversation

Tim Russert

Long-time American television journalist and long-serving Meet the Press moderator Tim Russert published an excellent book, *Big Russ and Me*, with many takeaways. He referred to a polite way to decline invitations that I adapted and still use continuously.

He discussed being invited to a party or event you do not feel comfortable saying no to. A close friend or family member may have asked you, someone you do not want to disappoint for whatever reason. His response's simplicity, politeness, and effectiveness are perfectly crafted, "Thank you very much for the invitation. I have a previous commitment, so I cannot attend."

- You acknowledge the invitation.
- Next, share you already have a previous commitment that I can't get out of.

This response made great sense with his political background and came across as more genuine and comfortable than "No. Sorry, can't go."

If you ever find yourself in this situation, give that response a shot. You will be surprised at how pleasant and gracious the experience turns out instead of rejecting the invitation differently.

CHAPTER 9

The Two Most Important Women in My Life

"A good wife is heaven's last, best gift to man - his gem of many virtues, his casket of jewels; her voice is sweet music, her smiles his brightest day, her kiss the guardian of his innocence, her arms the pale of his safety."
— *Jeremy Taylor*

The Impact of My Mother

'There is no greater name for a leader than mother or father. There is no leadership more important than parenthood.'
— *Sheri L. Dew.*

My mom recently passed in January 2024 after a long battle with her illness at 95 years young. Many people my age, and unfortunately those younger, can resonate with this point. The decision becomes, how can I best care for her the way she did for me? For some, the answer is assisted living.

On the other hand, many people urge their kids never to put them in a nursing home. What if the care is out of our financial reach, needing treatments for early-on sets of dementia or Alzheimer's?

The magnitude and weight of this decision is a heavy burden they put on their kids. In my mom's case, I never had to battle that.

You may also be able to resonate with this: the awkward and uncomfortable moment when you realize your mom or dad should not be behind the wheel anymore. With a delicate subject, I didn't know if there was a correct way to approach this.

- "Mom, you need to stop driving."
- Take away their keys.

My mother has been a widow for 20 years, and this last bit of control over her day was slowly evaporating.

She had seen a lot in her life, starting in Canada and ending in the United States. At one point, her original, large home in Maine was filled with kids and chaos. It eventually became too much to handle. The benefit, however, is that she was the one to recognize this. She also was the one to admit that it was in her best interest to move into an assisted living facility.

Mixed with emotions, I began slowly packing up box after box on multiple visits and listing the house on the market to help her with the burden of moving.

After coming to terms with these areas, the next area she decided to move on from was driving. She didn't want to fight it and knew it was just me. I was an only child for the most part— my half-brother is 15 years older than me, so the age difference limited our relationship, and I have never been remotely close with my half-sister. With larger families, there can be more arguments between multiple siblings with different opinions on what is best for their parents.

Now that I have the chance to reflect, it's funny how we take on specific characteristics of our parents.

I see myself and how I am in many ways with both of them.

My wife says I'm stubborn, a trait I inherited from my father. In contrast, my mother was calming and quiet, influencing my introversion. Like her, I'm constantly questioning and thinking.

When I look at how she influenced my life and her final years, I already have said if I can't take care of myself, bring me to an assisted living facility. I don't want them to have the burden of taking care of me. Another benefit of these facilities at an older age is you are in a community of people again for the first time in what may be many years or decades. My daughter works in the nursing field and sees much of this daily.

I have always admired my wife because she is calming, good-natured, and has a beautiful sense of humor while I'm serious. She's the good cop, and I'm the bad cop, with a hint of a good cop, too!

When she says, "Excuse me," she seems more caring. She can diffuse an agitated situation quickly and make light of it, handling it humorously and making it less adversarial. I'm jealous of this.

Flipping the script, my dad would have yelled and screamed, making a big deal of it and affecting everyone else. Their reactions were always "night and day" different. She taught me patience and how to react correctly in situations.

Pictured here is Mom. She had such a quiet impact on my life. By her actions, I learned so much from her and will miss her terribly. She passed on January 29, 2024

The Impact of My Wife

"Of all the home remedies, a good wife is best."
— Kin Hubbard

I read that chivalry is an act of selflessness stemming from a deeper part of oneself. It involves giving without expecting anything in return. This description perfectly encapsulates my wife.

My wife and I first crossed paths at McDonald's when I was transferred to the St. John Street location in Portland, Maine. At the time, she was 16, and I was 21. As she reached 18, our conversations evolved, deepening our friendship and turning our relationship more serious.

She is currently employed at St. Anselm College/AVI Food Service. Over the years, I have learned many of her peers at work look up to her and are motivated by her. Additionally, if she left her job there today, many people would follow suit or start looking for another job.

They may wait to quit, but they wouldn't be very pleased. My wife has always been a motivational force at work, and her departure would have consequences for the rest of the staff. She exemplifies maintaining a positive demeanor at work despite challenges and serving as a leader for colleagues.

She is the glue at her work; you would never know if she's having a bad day there. It can catch up when the work rush ends, and she has time to decompress or wake up the next day. In life, we often unload our problems on those closest to us.

We keep our cool all day, bottle it up, do what we must, and then the word vomit comes out. It happens to the best of us. If you show your cards at work that you're having a bad day, it takes your energy away.

The way my wife is with words and actions has always amazed me. If you bump into them while walking or cut in front of her driving, instead of getting mad, she brushes it off with a smile and laughs, "Don't worry about it!"

At the beginning of the school year, she worked 12-hour days, six days a week, because the company was short-staffed. Long days and not enough workers are often two panic buttons for employees.

You would never know if she's tired, grumpy, or even angry when she is short-handed with an extra workload. One way I can describe her is having admirable resiliency. She can rebound from any situation, whether it's a challenge with the relationship or at work.

She is truly the glue that holds it all together. I am not just making this up; In 2023, she was recognized with the incredible Walter Gallo Award for her dedication, service, and jovial work ethic. I want to share some of the remarks the event host gave:

"Terry serves with kindness. It's not uncommon to hear Terry comforting a homesick first-year student, congratulating a student-athlete on a well-won victory, or encouraging a nervous senior before their first job interview. Terry is also a model and a mentor to her fellow employees in the coffee shop.

Terry's always willing to listen and lend a helping hand. Terry continues to make a lasting impact on our campus. One of her nominees wrote: Her dedication and care of our students, alumni, faculty, the Monastic community, and staff is truly incredible. Her treatment of our students is sometimes indescribable. You have to witness her actions to see her impact on our students."

These words are kind but still do not do justice to how wonderful my wife is.

Terry and I pictured after her award-winning evening when she received the "Walter Gallo" award. It sounds a little "Cliché" but she has been with me since 1986. Her sense of making light of tense situation is admirable. The way she carries herself amongst her peers is amazing. She is truly a "Caring" individual. I wish I had half of her amazing traits.

CHAPTER 10

Putting It All Together

"Alone, we can do so little; together,
we can do so much."
— *Helen Keller*

Reflecting on concluding this book, I've realized how much McDonald's has positively impacted my life. I've absorbed and implemented numerous daily, weekly, and monthly life lessons that continue to guide me.

Today, as I finish this last chapter, I am sitting in on a training class for Manitowoc Ice to support a trainer during this presentation. I'm always thinking about how we could become better presenters as a company.

My life has evolved into a lifetime of teaching and holds experiences I will treasure and always think of.

This book was written to help you become a more robust and effective leader. In addition to my experiences, I introduced you to influential people, including Dale Carnegie, Ken Blanchard, and Steven Covey.

With Dale's teachings, I emerged from an introvert to find success and stay mindful of the importance of remembering and using names.

Through Ken's training principles, I led countless individuals to become the best version of themselves.

It brings me joy to continue sharing my wisdom with my granddaughter, Izzy. Earlier, we discussed the correct way to reject someone else's invitation, where you don't just say no but also acknowledge and appreciate the ask.

I picked her up early from work this weekend at 3:00 PM as she was scheduled from noon until 4:00 PM. She shared that her manager asked if she would like to leave early. Here I go, starting to influence my 15-year-old granddaughter. I can't stop. Tim Russert shows up again.

We had a conversation where I shared that she does not need to feel compelled to go home whenever her boss asks her. I continued and shared an option of what she could say instead: "Thank you for asking me if I want to go home early. I have no way to get home." Of course, I also encouraged her to avoid using the word "but" in her response.

Earlier, I expressed my pride in my daughter, who excels in her leadership role and effortlessly managed the soda machine. As she develops as a leader, my advice remains consistent: praise publicly and offer criticism privately.

When doing so, the team appreciates and respects you more. In turn, that leads to better results for the company. I stand by this: it is a poor leadership trait to make yourself look good at the expense of others.

Before signing off and wishing you well, I will summarize the book and leave you with closing tips to improve your leadership:

- Be part of the solution, not the problem, when it comes to company culture

- If you have a problem, offer a solution. If you don't have a solution for the problem, keep quiet.
- Don't be that person who is always complaining, you know who they are
- Successfully adapt to changes. Give change a chance, time usually makes the change better in the long run
- Listen to what your team is telling you
- Be open to feedback and coaching
- Effectively delegate assignments to the team members with the strengths required to excel.
- Improve communication skills
- Seek mentors and guidance
- Be empathetic and understanding
- Put yourself in your team member's shoes
- Praise in public, criticize in private
- Be firm but fair

That is all I have for you. What's next for me? I will continue to lead by example and enjoy life. I would love to connect with you. Search for my name on LinkedIn, and let's have a conversation.

Remember,

> *"The only safe ship in a storm is leadership."*
> *— Faye Wattleton*

Best wishes,
Charlie Newcomb

Recommended Reading

Ken Blanchard:
The One Minute Manager
The One Minute Manager Meets the Monkey
Zap The Gaps
Raving Fans
Who Moved My Cheese?

Rhonda Byme:
The Secret
James C. Collins
Good to Great

Ray & Joan Kroc:
The Man Who Made the McDonald's Fortune and the Woman
Who Gave It All Away

Tim Russert:
Big Russ & Me

Sources

Harvard Business

https://www.harvardbusiness.org/good-leadership-it-all-starts-with-trust/#:~:text=The%20Benefits%20of%20a%20High%2DTrust%20Organization&text=In%20contrast%2C%20employees%20at%20low,is%20slower%20and%20less%20effective

New York Times

https://www.nytimes.com/2017/01/20/your-money/ray-joan-kroc-mcdonalds-fortune-philanthropy.html

Forbes

https://www.forbes.com/sites/carolkinseygoman/2018/08/26/5-ways-body-language-impacts-leadership-results/